FIGHTERS

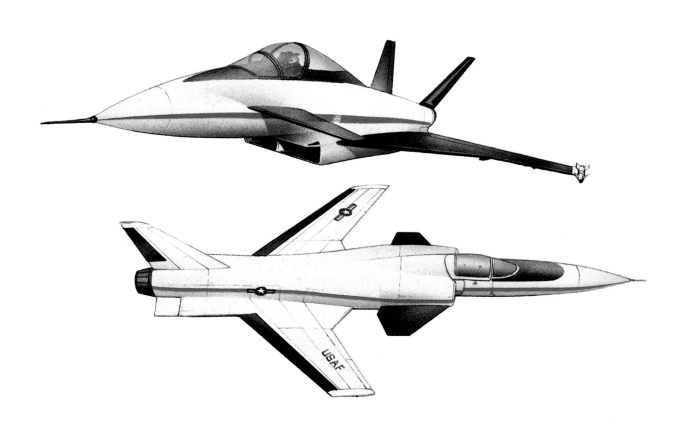

Modern Military Techniques

MODERN MILITARY TECHNIQUES
FIGHTERS

Malcolm V. Lowe

Illustrations by
Peter Sarson & Tony Bryan

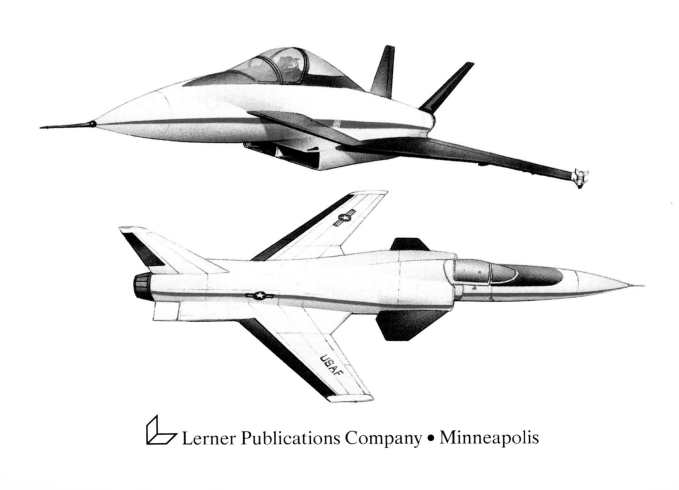

Lerner Publications Company • Minneapolis

This book is available in two editions:
Library binding by Lerner Publications Company
Soft cover by First Avenue Editions
241 First Avenue North
Minneapolis, Minnesota 55401

Library of Congress Cataloging in Publication Data

Lowe, Malcolm V.
  Fighters.

  (Modern military techniques)
  Includes index.
  Summary: A survey of today's fighter planes, their
design, equipment, and defense capabilities, with
information about future fighter developments.
  1. Fighter planes—Juvenile literature. 2. Jet
planes, Military—Juvenile literature. [1. Fighter
planes. 2. Airplanes, Military] I. Sarson, Peter, ill.
II. Bryan, Tony, ill. III. Title. IV. Series.
UG1242.F5L69 1985   358.4'3   84-7941
ISBN 0-8225-1376-5 (lib. bdg.)
ISBN 0-8225-9506-0 (pbk.)

Manufactured in the United States of America

7 8 9 10 11 12 13 14 15 16 99 98 97 96 95 94 93 92 91 90

CONTENTS

1
The Fighter in Modern Warfare

Like the fighter aircraft of the past, the modern fighter carries out a number of important roles. These are mainly defensive roles against hostile aircraft, but the fighter is also used to attack ground targets.

Interception

The interceptor is used to defend friendly airspace against intrusion by hostile aircraft (see pages 20, 21). The fighters should be ready to take off on a scramble and to intercept hostile fighters or bombers in the shortest possible time, so the fighters are kept in a state of readiness for their pilots by expert ground crews. The F-16 Fighting Falcon (see also pages 12, 13), shown here with its air-to-air missiles on the wing-tips, is also often deployed for air combat. Like many modern fighters, it can undertake a variety of tasks.

Deterrence

Fighters are sent up to find and shadow any potentially hostile aircraft transgressing friendly airspace: photographic reconnaissance spy planes, for example, or straying air-liners. Usually the fighter will escort the intruder away, but there is an internationally known code of signals by which the fighter pilot can instruct the aircraft to turn back or to land at a suitable airfield. Here, an F-4 Phantom is illustrated escorting away a Russian Tu-95 bomber.

Naval Defense

Fighters based on aircraft carriers are required to defend the aircraft carriers themselves and the ships of the Fleet to which they are attached. Also, when the other aircraft — the attack bombers for example — also based on the carriers, fly out on their missions, the fighters escort them so that they are immediately on hand for defense. Shown here, flying over its aircraft carrier, is an A-7 Corsair II, a multi-purpose aircraft capable of carrying a wide variety of bombs and missiles.

Ground Attack

An important role for the fighter is to attack ground targets, such as enemy tanks or airfields. Most fighter aircraft can carry the bombs and missiles required for this task in addition to the air-to-air missiles used in dog-fighting and interception. Here, an F-105 Thunderchief releases its load of bombs during a ground attack mission.

F-16 Fighting Falcon

Air Combat

Air combat fighters are essential to gain command of the air over enemy territory. To demonstrate their ability to gain air superiority, fighters must be capable of engaging in dog-fights with opposing fighters (see pages 16, 17). A Tornado is shown here dog-fighting with a Russian Su-24.

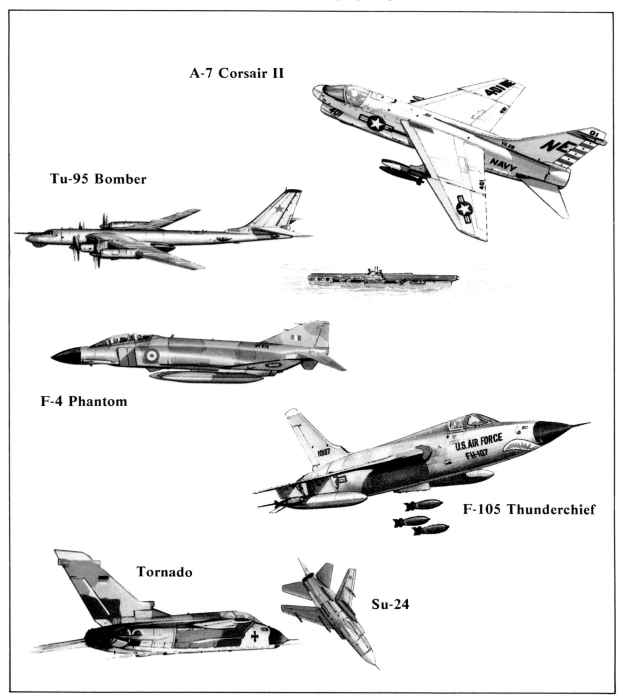

A-7 Corsair II

Tu-95 Bomber

F-4 Phantom

F-105 Thunderchief

Tornado

Su-24

2 Fighter Design Features (1)

Important primary roles that fighters have to carry out are air defense (interception) and air combat (dog-fighting). The fighter's major aim is to win air superiority and deny airspace to hostile aircraft, and often a fighter might be required to carry out either or both of these basic interception and dog-fighting roles. In many cases, however, the fighter's particular primary role is important in deciding its basic design.

1. Interceptor Features

Interceptors are necessary for the defense of large regions from intrusion by hostile aircraft, and they require great power to lift the long-range radar and missiles necessary to their roles. The interceptor may have to travel long distances to protect its country's airspace, so it must be very fast. It must have a streamlined shape, powerful engines, and a large fuel capacity. The wings may be relatively small, as the interceptor is not primarily designed to engage in dog-fighting. The F-15 Eagle illustrated here is a twin-finned, twin-engined single-seater with an exceptional performance record. Although it burns fuel at a phenomenal rate, it is regarded as one of the best fighters available for both interception and air combat duties.

2. Air Combat Features

Air combat fighters are used to gain command of the airspace inside enemy territory. They must be extremely agile for the tight turns of dog-fighting but do not usually need to carry the heavy long-

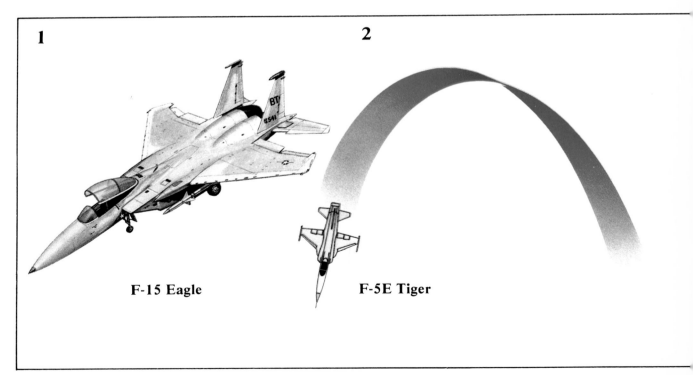

1

2

F-15 Eagle

F-5E Tiger

range radar and missiles of the interceptors, so they can be smaller. To be successful, the air combat fighter must be able to out-turn its opponent to bring it in firing range within the cone of vulnerability (see page 16).

3. Swing-Wing Designs

To fly very fast, a fighter aircraft should have a relatively small wingspan. But when carrying large bombloads, the aircraft normally requires a large wingspan in order to get airborne. The variable sweep or swing-wing designs have been evolved to give this flexibility. The wings are spread for take-off and landing and for cruising at sub-sonic speeds and then folded back for making a full throttle dash. With the wing sweep controlled automatically, the F-14 Tomcat variable geometry aircraft shown here can out-maneuver most previous designs of combat aircraft. The swing-wing design is particularly useful for naval aircraft. The fighters can land on their aircraft carriers at low speeds with the wings extended, and they can also fly air patrols over the Fleet with their wings set in this way, thus saving valuable fuel.

TOP FIGHTERS

General Dynamics F-16 Fighting Falcon

Data for F-16A Fighting Falcon
(see p. 12-13)

The Fighting Falcon first emerged in the early 1970s as a Light Weight Fighter demonstrator, subsequently becoming the world's best dog-fighting air combat fighter including features such as fly-by-wire controls and excellent avionics for attack and fighter missions. In U.S. front-line service, the F-16 partners the F-15 Eagle. Countries such as Egypt, South Korea, Pakistan, Venezuela, Israel, Belgium, Norway, Denmark, and the Netherlands have all bought the aircraft, the last four named countries participating in a European construction program in addition to the U.S. assembly lines.

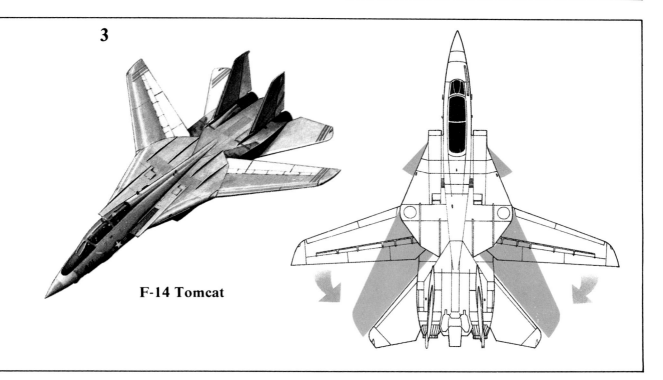

3

F-14 Tomcat

9

3 Fighter Design Features (2)

4. Special Features of the Harrier

The swiveling nozzles that enable the Harrier to make a vertical take-off can also be used to give the aircraft a marked advantage in dog-fighting. By rotating the nozzles downwards during forward flight, the pilot can reduce speed and still keep his aircraft under control. This technique is called VIFFing. Diagram 4 shows how the Harrier loses speed when the nozzles are vectored (rotated or directed downwards), allowing the pilot to get into a good firing position behind the Mirage. The Harrier is one of the few operational fighters able to fly in this way. Most other fighters have fixed jet outlets, usually in the tail, which cannot be rotated. As demonstrated during the Falkland Islands conflict, this feature gives the Harrier a significant advantage when engaging in air combat duties.

5. Radar Applications

The fighter's main radar is mounted in the aircraft's nose (5). This is very important in finding the fighter's opponents by day or night and in any weather conditions, although the type of radar used often depends on the aircraft's primary role. Interceptors carry heavy long-range radar, and sometimes, as with the F-14 Tomcat, a second crew member is carried to work the fighter's radar and avionics properly. Although Air Combat fighters do not have such long-range radar, it is still very effective. A rearward-looking receiver, often mounted in or around the tail (see illustration 5), warns of enemy aircraft trying to enter the fighter's cone of vulnerability (see page 16).

6. Delta Wing Designs

Mirage fighters belong to a group of planes developed by a French firm. Many of these Mirage fighters have a delta wing design that removes the necessity for the horizontal tailplane and gives a wing of low drag, enabling the fighter to move very efficiently through the air at speed. The additional room inside the wing gives increased fuel capacity (see diagram far right). As some pilots have found that the wing does not allow the tight turns of dog-fighting to be made easily, the later models carry small winglets near the nose to give increased lift. Picture 6 shows a Mirage III turning, while a Kfir — based on the air frame of a Mirage 5 — is able to make a much tighter turn because of its additional winglets.

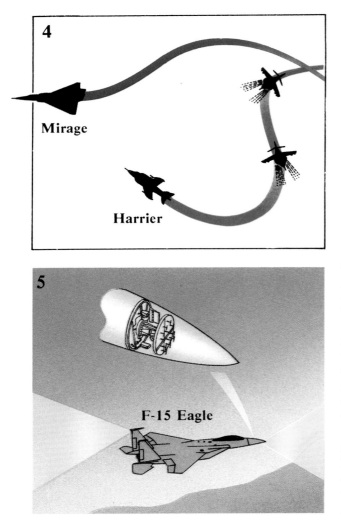

4

Mirage

Harrier

5

F-15 Eagle

TOP FIGHTERS

Dassault-Breguet Mirage III and 5/50 series

Data for Mirage IIIE

Dimensions: Span 8.22 m; Length 15.03 m; Height 4.50 m.
Power Plant: One SNECMA Atar 9C turbojet engine of 6,200 kg thrust with afterburner.
Performance: Maximum Speed 2,350 km/h or Mach 2.2 at 12,000 m; Combat radius (hi-lo-hi ground attack mission with external fuel) 1,200 km.
Armament: Two 30 mm DEFA cannons in fuselage, underfuselage and underwing pylons for 454 kg bombs and air-to-ground missiles, Matra R.530 or Matra Super 530 air-to-air missiles and Sidewinder or Matra 550 Magic dog-fighting missiles.

The Mirage III and 5/50 series of fighters and ground attack aircraft, with their distinctive delta wings, are some of the best-known and most widely used fighters currently in service. All versions have seen considerable export success, while the Mirage III and 5 also equip units of the French Armée de l'Air. The Mirage IIIE is a very capable fighter and ground attack aircraft in service with French and overseas squadrons. Mirages and Israeli-produced examples called Dagger saw action with Argentine forces during the 1982 Falkland Islands conflict, while the Israeli Air Force uses a developed version named Kfir.

6

Mirage III

Kfir

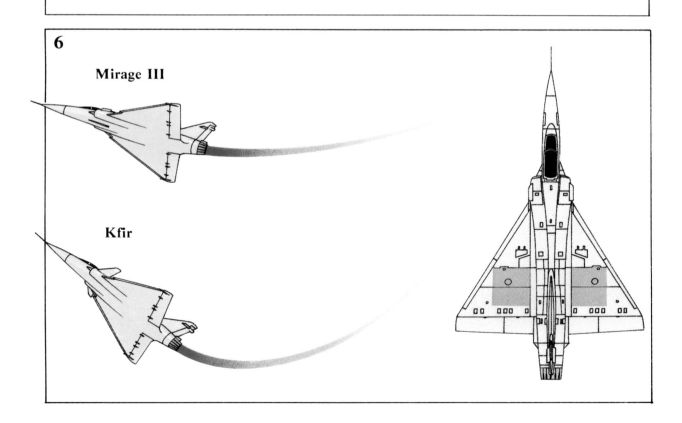

4
F-16A Fighting Falcon Air Combat Fighter

Specifications:

Wing span (including wing-tip missiles)	: 32 ft. 10 in. (10 m)
Length	: 49 ft. 6 in. (15.1 m)
Height (to tip of vertical tail)	: 16 ft. 5 in. (5 m)
Wing area	: 300 ft. (27.9 m^2)
Empty weight	: 15,140 lb. (6,870 kg)
Typical take-off weight (with 2 Sidewinder missiles for Air Combat mission)	: 23,810 lb. (10,800 kg)
Maximum speed	: 1,320 mph (2,112 km/h) or Mach 2.0
Service ceiling	: 60,000 ft.+ (18,290 m+)
Radius of action	: 575 miles (925 km)

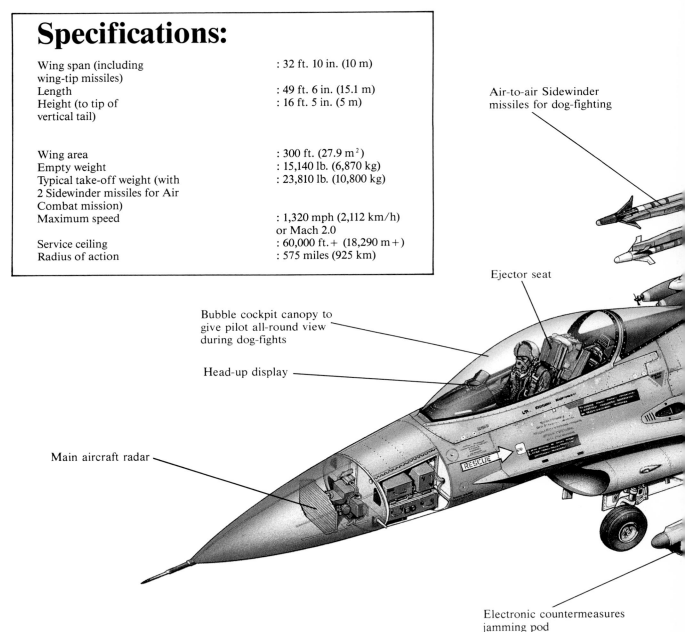

Air-to-air Sidewinder missiles for dog-fighting

Ejector seat

Bubble cockpit canopy to give pilot all-round view during dog-fights

Head-up display

Main aircraft radar

Electronic countermeasures jamming pod

This drawing displays the main features of the multi-purpose F-16A Fighting Falcon and shows the type of weapons and other stores that can be carried on the wing-tips and under the wings and fuselage of the fighter. In addition to its widespread use in the U.S. Air Force, the Fighting Falcon is used by air forces throughout the world. As well as being an excellent fighter for dog-fighting, the F-16 is a very capable ground attack aircraft. Here it is shown in a low-visibility color scheme (compare camouflage, pages 32, 33). The Fighting Falcon is an innovative design with some unusual new features. The pilot lies back in a reclining seat to counteract the effects of gravity and flies the plane by means of a side-stick control instead of the conventional control column.

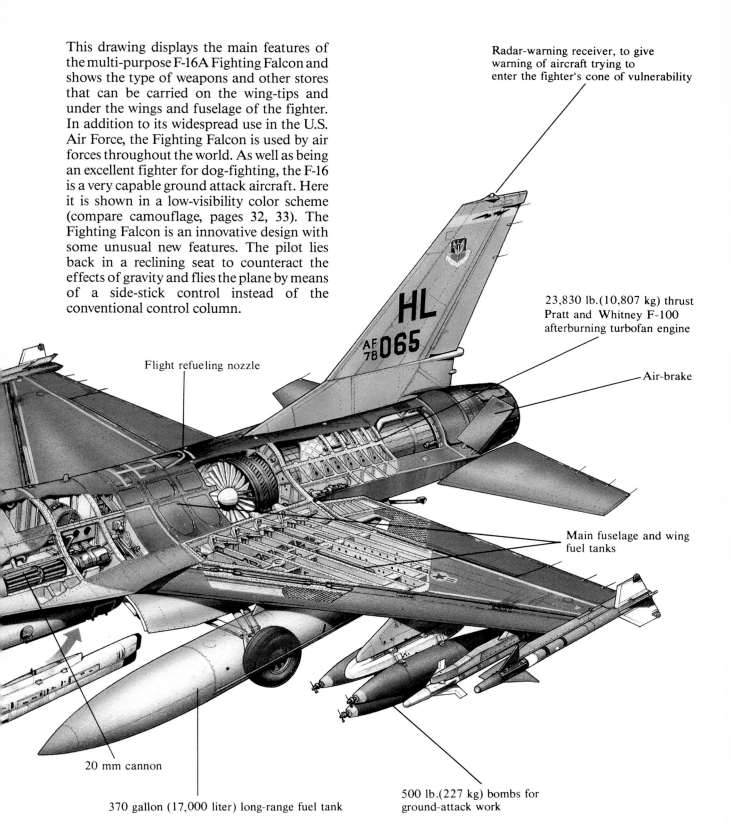

Radar-warning receiver, to give warning of aircraft trying to enter the fighter's cone of vulnerability

23,830 lb.(10,807 kg) thrust Pratt and Whitney F-100 afterburning turbofan engine

Air-brake

Main fuselage and wing fuel tanks

Flight refueling nozzle

20 mm cannon

370 gallon (17,000 liter) long-range fuel tank

500 lb.(227 kg) bombs for ground-attack work

13

5 Fighter Armament

Fighter Armament

In addition to traditional machine guns or cannon, modern fighters can carry a great variety and number of missiles and bombs, only a few examples of which are listed here. The cannon and air-to-air missiles are very important in interception and dog-fighting missions, while a number of air-to-ground bombs can be carried for ground attack work.

Air-to-Air Missiles

Interceptors usually carry long-range missiles that can be fired at their opponents at great range in all weather conditions. The fighter carries a fire control system — which includes the large long-range radar — to ensure that these missiles strike their target. This radar locks onto the enemy aircraft at long range and guides the missile to it; the radar seeker within the missile (see diagram 2)

1   F-14 Tomcat

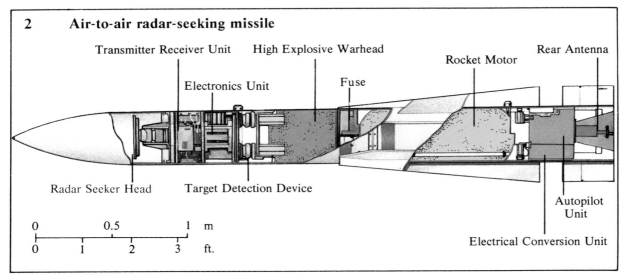

2   Air-to-air radar-seeking missile

Transmitter Receiver Unit   High Explosive Warhead   Rear Antenna

Electronics Unit   Fuse   Rocket Motor

Radar Seeker Head   Target Detection Device

Autopilot Unit

Electrical Conversion Unit

| 0 | | 0.5 | | 1 | m |
| 0 | 1 | 2 | 3 | | ft. |

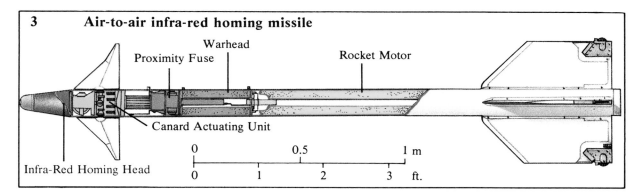

3 Air-to-air infra-red homing missile

Proximity Fuse

Warhead

Rocket Motor

Canard Actuating Unit

Infra-Red Homing Head

0   0.5   1 m

0   1   2   3   ft.

helps guide it directly to the target. In illustration 1, an F-14 Tomcat fires its Phoenix interception missile, which has a maximum range of over 99 miles (160 km).

Dog-fighting missiles only require a shorter range, and often a large radar is not necessary to guide them to the target. Instead, they have an infra-red homing device in the nose (see diagram 3). When the missile is fired, this homes in on the infra-red radiation/heat given out by the target, and the forward fins move to maneuver the missile onto its target.

Air-to-Ground Weapons

Free-fall unguided bombs, like the Fighting Falcon's 500 lb. bombs in the cutaway drawing on pages 12-13, are often used for ground attack. These are not usually as accurate as guided weapons, which are homed onto their targets by various means including radar in the weapon's nose, infra-red homing, and laser guidance. The laser-equipped weapon in illustration 4 uses its

nose-mounted detector to pick out the target. Friendly ground forces or a Forward Air Control aircraft, for example, illuminate the target for the detector using laser guidance.

TOP FIGHTERS

Grumman F-14 Tomcat

Data for F-14A Tomcat

Dimensions: Span (wings fully swept-back) 11.65 m, (wings fully spread) 19.55 m; Length 19.10 m; Height 4.88 m.
Power Plant: Two Pratt & Whitney TF30-P-412A turbofan engines of 9,480 kg thrust with afterburner.
Performance: Maximum Speed (with four Sparrow missiles) 2,485 km/h or Mach 2.34 at 12,190 m; Combat Radius (with four Sparrow missiles and internal fuel) 725 km.
Armament: One 20 mm M61 multi-barrel cannon in fuselage, provision for combinations of Sidewinder, Sparrow, and Phoenix air-to-air missiles, up to 6,575 kg of air-to-ground weapons.

The swing-wing Tomcat was a huge step forward in the U.S. Navy's fighter capability when it became operational during the earlier 1970's. It is the only fighter in the world to operationally carry weapons ranging from internal cannon right up to the long-range Phoenix missile.

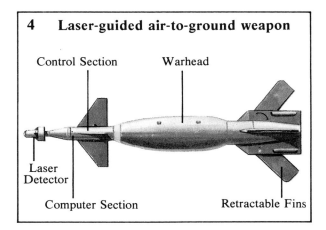

4   Laser-guided air-to-ground weapon

Control Section

Warhead

Laser Detector

Computer Section

Retractable Fins

6 Fighter Combat Tactics

Aerial combat is the most important action for which fighter aircraft and their weapons are designed. In close air combat, the fighter pilot has a number of movements that he can use either to defend himself from the attacking fighter or to attempt to drive away his attacker himself. The movements used by jet fighters in modern aerial dog-fights have changed little from those used in the Second World War by aircraft like the Spitfire and Messerschmitt, except that the aircraft speeds are now much greater. Modern targeting methods give the fighter pilot more flexibility in firing his weapons (see pages 22-23).

1 A Fighter Aircraft's Cone of Vulnerability

If an attacking aircraft, shown here on the right, is able to fly into the cone-shaped area of sky behind a fighter aircraft, its pilot is able to fire his weapons at his opponent with a good chance of hitting him. The defending fighter pilot, on the left, must therefore make sure that an attacker does not fly into this area of sky behind him.

2 The "Defensive Break"

This shows the possible movements for a defending fighter pilot if he sees that his opponent is approaching his cone of vulnerability. He can dive away in a tight turn while his attacker, who cannot tell when he is going to turn, flies past him and loses his chance to attack.

3 "High Speed Yo-Yo"

Here the attacking aircraft on the right turns inside a defensive break. His tight turn allows him to dive after the defending fighter so that he can get back into his original attacking position.

4 The "Scissors" Maneuver

Each aircraft turns around the other, the defending fighter on the left trying to slow down so that his attacker will fly past him. He can then fly into his attacker's own cone of vulnerability.

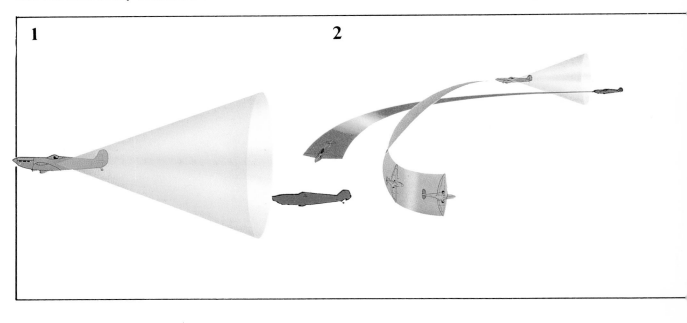

1 2

TOP FIGHTERS

British Aerospace (Hawker Siddeley) Harrier/Sea Harrier

Data for Sea Harrier FRS.Mk.1

Dimensions: Span 25 ft. 3 in. (7.70 m); Length 47 ft. 7 in. (14.50 m); Height 12 ft. 2 in. (3.70 m).
Power Plant: One Rolls Royce Pegasus 104 vectored-thrust turbofan of 21,500 lb. (9,752 kg) thrust.
Performance: Maximum Speed over 720 mph (1,160 km/h) or Mach 0.95 at 1,000 ft. (305 m); Tactical Radius (intercept mission with external fuel, two 30 mm cannons and two Sidewinders) 450 miles (725 km).
Armament: All weapons carried externally, with underfuselage and underwing hardpoints for approximately 5,000 lb. (2,268 kg). Two 30 mm Aden cannons below fuselage, plus Sidewinder air-to-air dog-fighting missiles and air-to-ground and air-to-surface weapons.

The Harrier was the world's first V/STOL aircraft to enter operational service, representing a considerable technological development in combat aircraft. Its special vectored-thrust swivelling nozzles enable it to employ the technique called VIFFing, a great advantage in dog-fighting. The British Royal Navy version is the Sea Harrier, which successfully saw combat together with RAF Harriers in the 1982 Falkland Islands conflict. A developed version, the AV-8A/C, is in service with the U.S. Marine Corps, while India and Spain also use the type. Future developments include a possible supersonic version.

3   4

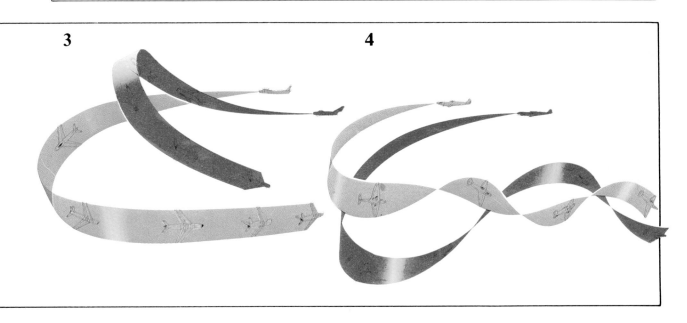

7
Fighter Combat Formations

Combat formations are used most by fighters in the air combat role, where dog-fighting demands a good all-round search ability to spot enemy fighters and provide mutual support. Important combat formations are shown here.

1 "Finger Four"

The four aircraft element is spread out resembling the positions of the finger-tips of an outstretched right hand. This formation allows each fighter room to maneuver if a defensive break is needed. It also makes it easy for each wing-man to move into fighting position behind his leader.

2 Fighting Position: Pair

During air fighting, the wing-man moves behind and off to one side of his leader, sometimes up to 35 degrees from his leader's line of flight. He follows his leader, watching and defending his leader's tail and cone of vulnerability, while his leader concentrates on attacking hostile fighters.

3 Battle Formation: Pair

Fighters will often enter combat in a pair. This line-abreast formation allows each pilot to view across, forward, and behind, thus providing good mutual support to avoid surprise and rear attacks. Fighters on a Combat Air Patrol may also adopt this formation.

4 "Fluid Four"

This is quite an open formation, comprising two basic elements of two fighters each: the two element leaders are at the front scanning forward, with their wing-men behind and to the sides scanning across the formation and to the rear. The formation, therefore, has a good all-round view. Typically, the two elements can be about 10,000 ft. (3,000 m) apart, with around 1,000 ft. (300 m) between the two aircraft of an element.

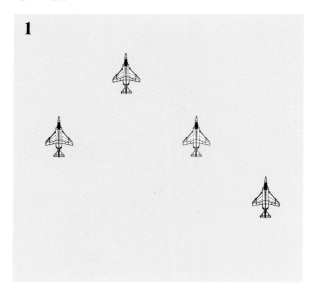

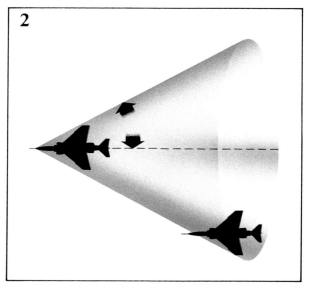

TOP FIGHTERS
Saab Viggen

Data for Saab JA37 Viggen

Dimensions: Span 10.60 m; Length (excluding nose probe) 15.45 m; Height 5.90 m.

Power Plant: One Volvo Flygmotor RM 8B turbofan engine of 12,750 kg thrust with afterburner.

Performance: Maximum Speed over 2,125 km/h or Mach 2 above 11,000 m; Combat Radius (intercept mission with AAMs) 400 km.

Armament: One 30 mm Oerlikon KCA cannon, up to six Sky Flash and Sidewinder air-to-air missiles, plus air-to-ground weapons.

The JA 37 Viggen is one of the most important fighters produced by countries other than the Superpowers. It contains the latest avionics and pilot displays, as well as an advanced L.M. Ericsson pulse-doppler radar for interception missions, and will fulfil Sweden's needs for a first-rate fighter able to meet any aggressor until at least the later 1990's.

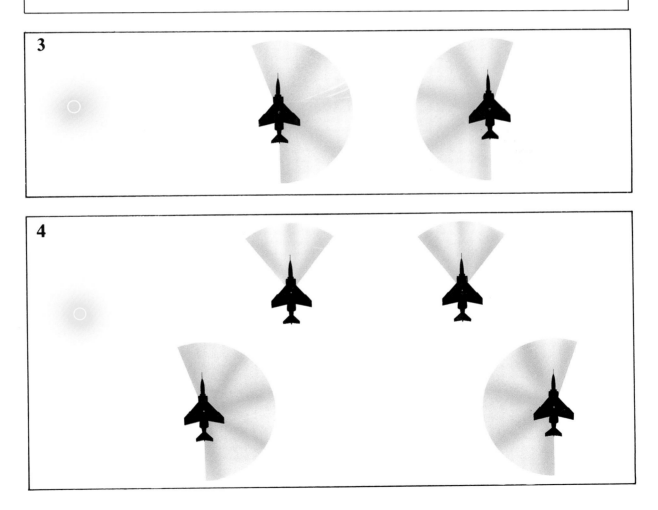

8 Elements of a Fighter Interception Mission

The fighter's role, to deny airspace to hostile fighters and bombers, is usually carried out in air combat, which aims to defeat and drive away the enemy aircraft. Sometimes, however, especially in peace-time, the mere presence of the fighter may be enough to deter the opposing aircraft from trying to enter friendly airspace.

In an interception mission, early warning of the attacking fighters and bombers is essential. The Airborne Early Warning aircraft (1) contains sophisticated radar that can detect enemy aircraft even when they are taking off from their own airfields (2). Ground radar carries out its warning function (3), while reconnaissance satellites (4) can survey the whole picture and give further information.

Warnings of the appearance of hostile aircraft are radioed to the friendly airbases, where fighters are scrambled to intercept the enemy as soon as possible (5). If the fighters are flying a Combat Air Patrol, they will be in the air already and therefore able to respond even faster. The fighter's own radar is powerful enough to detect the hostile aircraft at some range, and its pilot can receive further detailed information from the ground.

The interceptor is designed to engage the enemy at long distance with its long-range missiles. Very often, however, it is necessary to approach to close-range in order to identify the enemy aircraft properly or to ensure that they have hostile intentions before firing at them because IFF equipment is often unable to distinguish correctly between friend and enemy. Fighters tasked with the air combat role will dog-fight with enemy fighters if necessary in order to gain air superiority (6).

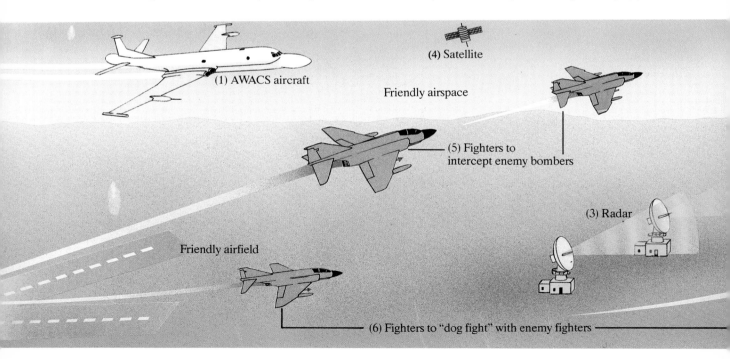

(4) Satellite

(1) AWACS aircraft

Friendly airspace

(5) Fighters to intercept enemy bombers

(3) Radar

Friendly airfield

(6) Fighters to "dog fight" with enemy fighters

TOP FIGHTERS

Mikoyan-Gurevich MiG-25 "Foxbat"

Data for MiG-25 "Foxbat-A"

Dimensions: Span 13.95 m; Length 23.82 m; Height 6.10 m.
Power Plant: Two Tumansky R-31 turbojet engines of 11,000 kg thrust with afterburner.
Performance: Maximum Speed 2,980 km/h or Mach 2.8 above 10,975 m; Combat Radius (with allowance for Mach 2.5 interception) 400 km.
Armament: No internal armament, wing pylons for (usually) four AA-6 "Acrid" AAMs (two infra-red homing, two semi-active radar homing).

The MiG-25 is one of the world's fastest aircraft, built to intercept the North American B-70 Valkyrie supersonic bomber. The bomber never became operational, but the appearance of the MiG-25 and its phenomenal performance helped lead to the creation of such fighters as the F-15 Eagle to counter it. The "Foxbat-A" is a true interceptor, without the agility needed for dog-fighting, and some versions are configured for fast and high reconnaissance; the type has been exported to countries such as Libya. The "Foxbat" can reach 3,400 km/h (Mach 3.2) with modified engines and has beaten many speed and height world records.

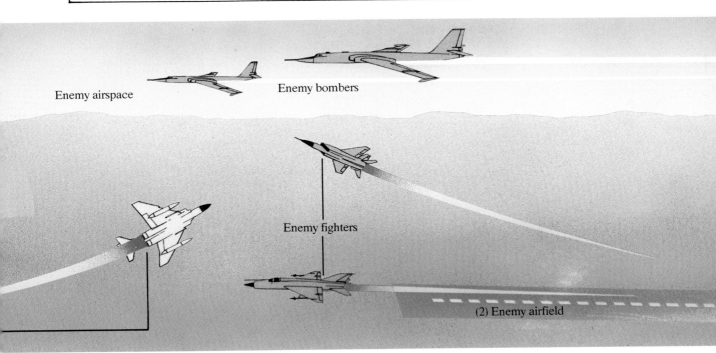

Enemy airspace

Enemy bombers

Enemy fighters

(2) Enemy airfield

9 Weapon Sighting

Fighters often carry fast-firing cannons, which are very useful in close air combat. A gunsight, positioned at the front of the cockpit ahead of the pilot, is used to sight the fighter's guns, although Head-Up Displays can also perform this task. In dog-fights, the pilot tries to fly into his opponent's cone of vulnerability, for here he has the target directly in front of him flying on the same course, where it is easiest to hit. Gunsights show the pilot when to fire, even if he cannot enter this cone of vulnerability. In close air combat, fighter pilots prefer to fire their guns or launch their heat-seeking missiles from within the opponent's cone of vulnerability. Most heat-seeking weapons have to be fired from this position; their success depends upon being able to home in on the heat given out by the opposing aircraft's engine, which is often best detected from behind or around its tail.

1 Head-Up Display (HUD)

A continuously computed impact line on the glass screen in front of the pilot shows where the aircraft's guns would strike; the central dot displays where the guns are sighted at any particular instant. The straight lines indicate the target's wingspan at various distances, important for judging range. The HUD can also show on its screens, when necessary, details of the fighter's own speed and other flight information. The pilot thus does not need to keep glancing down at his normal instruments in the cockpit but can keep his head up, allowing him to see where he is going and who he is chasing.

2 Gyro Gunsight

Here the gyro in the sight's mechanism positions the aiming dot, while the six-diamond circle can be sized in order to fit the target's wingspan to give range information. The gunsight shows the pilot when to fire if the target is moving at an angle to his fighter, displaying how far ahead the guns have to be fired so that their bullets will hit the target. This is necessary because otherwise, due to its speed, the target would fly away from the bullets if they were fired directly at it on the angle. The deflection angle is shown to the pilot by the gunsight, ensuring that his guns are fired in such a way that the target flies

into their line of flight. Such aiming systems as this allow the fighter pilot to fire at his opponent even when he is not within the target's cone of vulnerability. This is very useful, because the pilot may be unable to get into the favored position directly behind the target if, for example, he is firing at a number of targets in a short space of time.

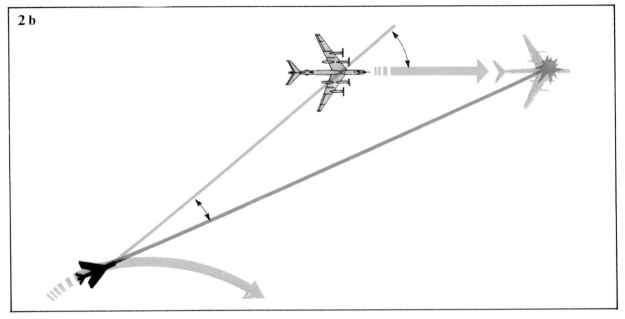

2 b

TOP FIGHTERS

Mikoyan-Gurevich MiG-23 "Flogger"

Data for MiG-23MF "Flogger-B"

Dimensions: Span (wings fully swept-back) 8.17 m, (wings fully spread) 14.25 m; Length (including nose probe) 16.80 m; Height 4.35 m.
Power Plant: One Tumansky R-29B turbofan engine of 12,475 kg thrust with afterburner.
Performance: Maximum Speed approximately 2,500 km/h or Mach 2.35 above 11,000 m; Combat Radius (air-to-air mission with internal fuel and four AAMs) 850 km.
Armament: One 23 mm GSh-23L cannon on underfuselage centerline, two AA-7 "Apex" medium-range and two AA-8 "Aphid" short-range air-to-air missiles.
Since its service introduction in the early 1970's, the MiG-23 has become established as a major fighter in the Soviet air force's inventory, being the most numerous type distributed in that service's Air Defense Force and Frontal Aviation. Like a small number of Western fighters, the "Flogger" is a swing-wing aircraft, and has been exported to several Warsaw Pact and overseas countries. The "Flogger-B" carries a large multi-mode nose intercept radar called "High Lark," with a search range of some 85 km; other versions of the MiG-23 are optimised for ground attack, as is the similar MiG-27.

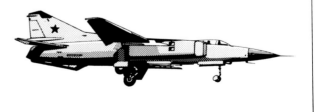

10 Ground Attack

A common type of attack mission that a fighter might carry out is a Close Air Support mission to aid friendly ground forces. Such attacks are made close to these ground forces, so the bombs must be dropped accurately. Another type of attack mission is carried out much further behind the enemy lines. Often, however, this particular type of mission is made by aircraft specially designed for ground attack work, and not necessarily by fighters. Even though the fighter might carry a large number of bombs on an attack mission, it will still carry some air-to-air missiles for air combat in case it meets enemy fighters (see pages 14-15).

Attacks using Special Weapons

Attack missions are sometimes made against enemy airfields. In this instance, the special type of weapon used is slowed by parachute when dropped, allowing the fighter to be well away from

the explosion when it occurs. A special rocket motor in the weapon helps it to dig into the runway and explode underneath, thus causing much damage.

Close Air Support

The fighter usually begins its attack from an Initial Point — often a prominent landmark — from which the attack sequence is carried out. After a specially timed run, the fighter turns onto a heading that leads directly to the target (aircraft B). This sequence helps to make sure that the fighter arrives at the target as planned. Sometimes, fluorescent ground panels can help guide the pilot, or markers such as smoke bombs can be fired by friendly infantry or a Forward Air Control aircraft to show where the target is. When a target is very close to friendly forces, however, an attack is made on a bomb line parallel to the line of battle to try to avoid hitting friendly positions (aircraft A).

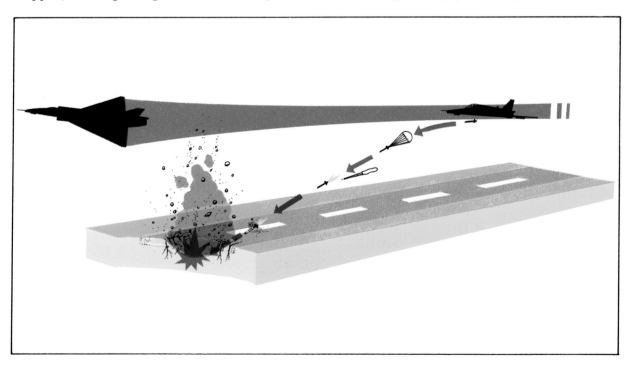

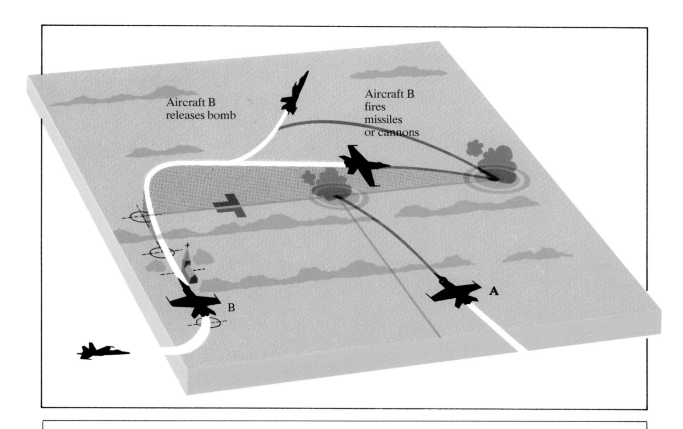

Aircraft B
releases bomb

Aircraft B
fires
missiles
or cannons

A

B

TOP FIGHTERS

Sukhoi Su-15 "Flagon"

Data for Su-15 "Flagon-F"

Dimensions (estimated): Span 10.53 m; Length 20.50 m; Height 5.0 m.
Power Plant: Two Tumansky R-13FD-300 turbojet engines of 6,600 kg thrust with afterburner.
Performance: Maximum Speed 2,660 km/h or Mach 2.5 at over 10,975 m; Combat Radius (at high altitude with AAMs) 725 km.
Armament: No internally mounted weapons, provision for carrying an underfuselage cannon pack of 23 mm weapons, AA-3 "Anab" air-to-air missiles below the wings and fuselage.

Since its operational debut in 1969-70, the Su-15 has been one of the most important front-line Russian fighters, performing as an all-weather interceptor and with a performance making it one of the fastest fighters in operation anywhere in the world. A continuous upgrading of its equipment has ensured a fully current fit of electronic warfare and other systems. As a part of the Soviet air force's Air Defense Force, the "Flagon" is a major component of a large and fully integrated system of interceptors, ground-control radars, and surface-to-air missiles that aim to provide a complete defense network against possible air attack.

11 Elements of a Fighter Attack Mission

Fighter attack missions are often flown to provide support for the main ground forces. In the drawing below, the friendly ground forces are shown on the left and the enemy land forces are on the right. Choice of targets for the fighters to attack can be made by examination of photographs of enemy positions taken by the photographic reconnaissance aircraft shown here flying high up above the enemy forces (1). Sub-variants of normal fighters may be produced especially for photographic reconnaissance, and these are fitted with special pods containing surveillance cameras (as shown on page 28). The pictures received by these cameras (opposite left) can then be enlarged by computer enhancement techniques to give a much higher resolution image (opposite right) from which experts can distinguish and accurately locate potential targets, such as military installations, enemy airfields, and missile silos. In addition, targets can be selected by the friendly ground units or by a Forward Air Control aircraft flying close to the lines of battle (2). This aircraft is usually a slow-flying light airplane from which the crew can easily spot targets. The disadvantage of these aircraft is that they are particularly vulnerable to enemy ground fire, and so close reconnaissance is sometimes made by un-manned remotely piloted vehicles. Further information is provided by reconnaissance satellites (3) making a general surveillance of the battlefield.

Once the targets have been found, details of their location and other information relevant to the attack are given to the fighter crews during a pre-flight briefing at their airbases (4). Airfields are usually safely behind the front line, so the fighters might be in the air already, fully armed and

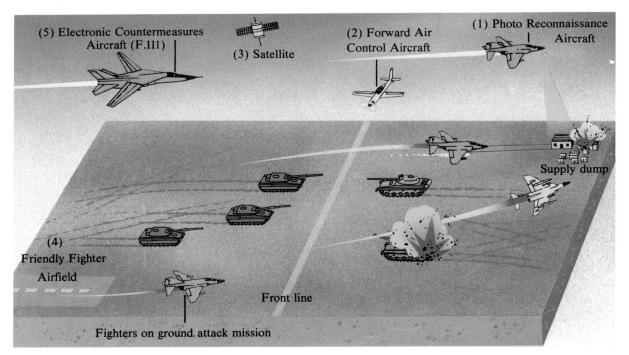

(5) Electronic Countermeasures Aircraft (F.111)

(3) Satellite

(2) Forward Air Control Aircraft

(1) Photo Reconnaissance Aircraft

Supply dump

(4) Friendly Fighter Airfield

Front line

Fighters on ground attack mission

awaiting instructions to fly to the battlefield. The vertical take-off Harrier can be based much closer to the battleground because it does not need a conventional airfield.

During their attack missions, fighters can be accompanied by an Electronic Countermeasures aircraft, but they also carry their own electronic warfare equipment. The Electronic Countermeasures aircraft (5) flies at a distance from the battle area, helping to confuse the enemy radars, which would otherwise be able to detect the attacking fighters.

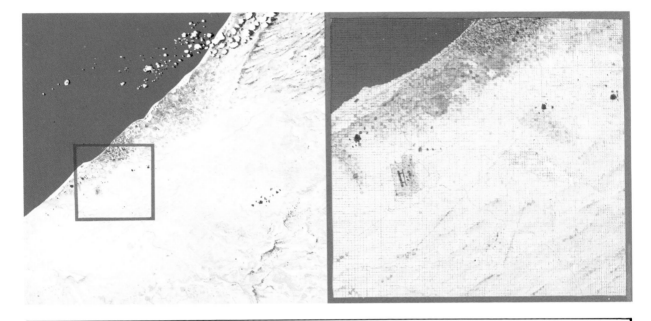

TOP FIGHTERS

McDonnell Douglas F/A-18 Hornet

Data for F-18A Hornet

Dimensions: Span (with wing-tip missiles) 40 ft. 4¾ in. (12.31 m); Length 56 ft. (17.07 m); Height 15 ft. 3½ in. (4.66 m).

Power Plant: Two General Electric F404-GE-400 turbofan engines of 16,000 lb. (7,260 kg) thrust with afterburner.

Performance: Maximum Speed 1,190 mph (1,915 km/h) or Mach 1.8 above 36,000 ft. Combat Radius (air-to-air mission on internal fuel) 460 miles (740 km).

Armament: One 20 mm Gatling rotary cannon in fuselage, provision for carrying Sidewinder dog-fighting missiles and Sparrow medium-range air-to-air missiles, plus combinations of missiles and bombs under wings and fuselage up to 17,000 lb. (7,710 kg) for ground attack.

The Hornet is the latest fighter to enter service with the U.S. Navy and Marine Corps, having an impressive air-to-air capability coupled with a high-power nose radar allowing it to engage enemy aircraft at medium range as well as being able to dog-fight very effectively. This air-to-air capacity has helped lead to some important export sales to Canada, Australia, and Spain. The aircraft also carries a large payload of air-to-ground ordnance, its internal avionics allowing the pilot to perform ground attack as well as fighter missions with considerable ease.

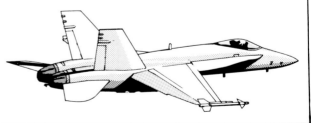

12 Photographic Reconnaissance

Photographic reconnaissance is an important part of the surveillance of battlefields and enemy positions, and vital in helping to select targets for fighters and attack aircraft. Many fighters are capable of being converted into reconnaissance machines; their speed is useful in allowing them to escape from enemy fighters because reconnaissance aircraft are often unarmed. Sometimes a sub-variant of a normal fighter is produced from the start for photographic duties, like the RF-5E shown below. A common type of reconnaissance installation has various downward- and sideways-looking cameras and sensors built into the nose of the fighter. Special pods can also be carried under the aircraft, which perform a similar function. The diagram illustrates a typical installation of a reconnaissance aircraft's cameras; the sideways-looking cameras, cameras 3 and 4 in the diagram, can scan from horizon to horizon.

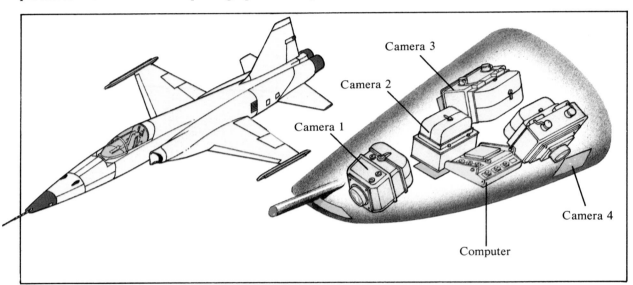

Radar Jamming

Equipment to confuse and jam enemy radar is very important if the fighter is to carry out its mission without being intercepted and attacked. In the picture opposite, (a) shows how easily the fighter can be detected by enemy radar if no jamming is used. In (b) the Electronic Countermeasures aircraft has used its transmitters to jam the opposing radars. Fighters also carry electronic countermeasures equipment, but it is not quite so powerful as the vast amount of equipment on board the jamming aircraft. To confuse enemy radar, fighters can also simply drop decoy flares and "chaff" — clouds of aluminized fiberglass or foil — because radars cannot distinguish between an actual fighter and this type of decoy. Chaff is a simple means of confusing enemy radars that has been in use very successfully since the Second World War.

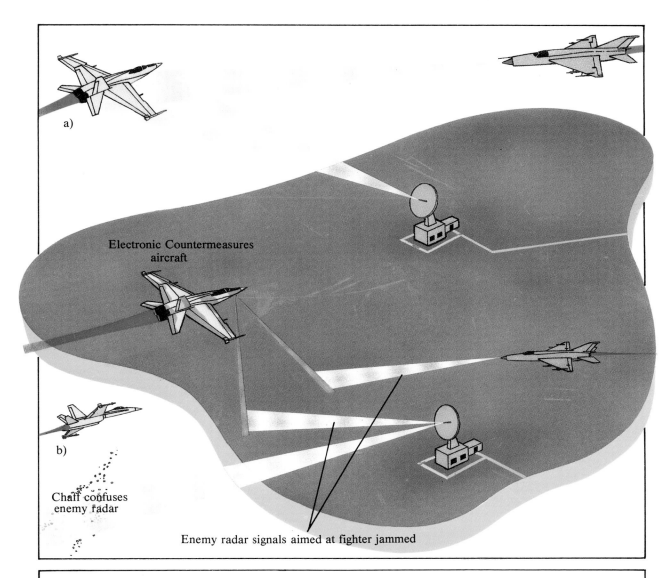

a)

Electronic Countermeasures
aircraft

b)

Chaff confuses
enemy radar

Enemy radar signals aimed at fighter jammed

TOP FIGHTERS

Dassault-Breguet Mirage 2000

Data for Mirage 2000

Dimensions: Span 9.0 m; Length 14.35 m; Height 5.30 m.

Power Plant: One SNECMA M53-5 bypass turbojet (low-ratio turbofan) of 9,000 kg thrust with afterburner.

Performance: Maximum Speed 2,350 km/h or Mach 2.2 above 11,000 m; Combat Radius (interception mission with external fuel) 700 km.

Armament: Two 30 mm DEFA cannons in fuselage, two Matra 550 Magic dog-fighting missiles and two Matra Super 530 air-to-air missiles.

Although bearing the name and a strong resemblance to the earlier delta Mirages, the 2000 is a new aircraft with the very latest design technology and systems, which will make it a formidable fighter for many years to come. It carries fly-by-wire flight controls allowing it to fly even in an unstable condition, and later production models will carry RDI pulse-doppler interception radar.

13 Long-Range Missions and Deployment

Sometimes, fighters have to operate many miles from their home bases, perhaps during an emergency to help a friendly country without too much equipment of its own. Some countries, therefore, have equipment available that can help their fighters travel great distances to the trouble-spot, and provide them with the material necessary to operate properly when they arrive.

A fighter's range is increased by carrying long-range fuel tanks under the wings (see diagram on page 11). Sometimes, however, even with these the aircraft cannot fly far enough to reach the trouble-spot. Many fighters can therefore be refuelled *during* flight. A fuel-tanker aircraft drops a fuel line down to the fighter, which carries a flight refuelling nozzle in a retractable arm on the upper surfaces of the fuselage. Fuel is transferred as the two aircraft fly along linked together. Illustration (1) shows a Tornado multi-role combat aircraft being refuelled in flight by a Royal Air Force Victor K.2 tanker aircraft. Considerable flying skill is required to line up the fighter aircraft so that the refuelling nozzle locks onto the fuel line.

Some aircraft carriers are large enough to contain several squadrons of aircraft. On United States Navy aircraft carriers, for example, two fighter squadrons may be deployed — in addition to the units of attack aircraft carried by the ship. Among other roles, the fighters provide escorts for the other aircraft when they fly their missions, as well as defending the carrier and other Navy ships in the Fleet from attack by hostile aircraft. As the take-off area on the carrier's flight deck is much shorter than normal runways on land, a powerful catapult is required to launch aircraft from the ship.

1

Aircraft carriers can sail thousands of miles from their home ports and carry their aircraft to almost any destination. They contain all the fuel, ammunition, and maintenance equipment needed to operate their aircraft properly. Below the flight deck are hangars where aircraft can be stored and worked on. To allow many aircraft to be parked on the flight deck, naval fighters have wings that fold up to give more room (3).

During the Falkland Islands conflict, Harriers of the British Task Force's carriers, were supplemented by others that were brought to the battle area by ordinary container ships. With their vertical take-off abilities (see page 10), the Harriers were able to fly off these ships when they arrived, even though the ships had no proper flight deck (2).

Radar, airfield defense systems, and other equipment had also been brought to the area to help the aircraft operate properly.

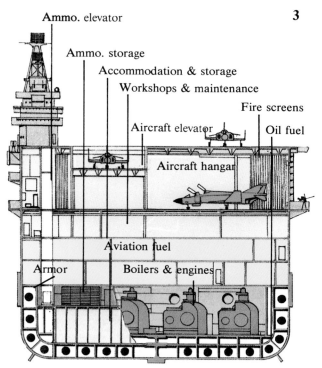

(see page 10)

TOP FIGHTERS

Yakovlev Yak-36 "Forger"

Data for Yak-36MP "Forger-A"

Dimensions (estimated): Span 7.50 m; Length 16.0 m; Height 3.35 m.
Power Plant: One Lyulka AL-21 lift/cruise turbojet of 8,000 kg thrust, plus two lift turbojets of some 3,600 kg thrust.
Performance (estimated): Maximum Speed of 1,120 km/h or Mach 1.05 above 10,975 m; Combat Radius (internal fuel and over 900 kg of air-to-surface weapons) 370 km.
Armament: No internal weapons, four underwing pylons for approximately 1,000 kg of bombs and other attack weapons, AA-8 "Aphid" short-range AAMs.

The Yak-36 is currently the only operational combat aircraft other than the BAe Harrier or its derivatives to include a vertical take-off and landing capability. The aircraft is a shipboard fighter and attack type and is totally unique in having only a VTOL capability, being unable to perform a normal rolling take-off. About a dozen are deployed aboard the Soviet ships Kiev, Minsk, and Novorossiisk, performing such tasks as fleet defense, reconnaissance, and anti-shipping missions; they are the only operational fixed-wing Soviet carrier-based aircraft.

14 Camouflage

When a fighter goes into action, it is very important that some form of concealment is used on its upper and lower surfaces to make it more difficult for the enemy to spot. Most air forces use a camouflage of drab colors to achieve this.

Camouflage schemes are usually designed to suit the type of environment in which the aircraft flies. In picture 1, the fighter's blue colors do not blend into the desert background but make the aircraft more easily seen. They are thus not suitable for use in the desert but can be used in areas where they help the fighter to blend into the background, for example, over water, as in picture 2.

Fighters flying in arid, desert areas use light colors (picture 3). Those operating in areas where there are many trees and fields, for example in Northern Europe, use dark shades, usually of greens and greys, to blend into that particular background (picture 4). Navy fighters often employ shades of grey, which blend well with the colors of the sea over which they are most likely to operate (picture 5). The fighter's undersurfaces are usually painted in a light shade, sometimes light blue (picture 6), to allow them to blend into the sky when the aircraft is seen from the ground. Recently, some air forces have adopted "low visibility" color schemes — as shown on the F-16A cutaway drawing on pages 12-13. This camouflage scheme makes the aircraft difficult to see when flying against several different backgrounds.

TOP FIGHTERS

British Aerospace (English Electric) Lightning

Data for Lightning F.Mk.6

Dimensions: Span 34 ft. 10 in. (10.61 m); Length (with nose probe) 55 ft. 3 in. (16.84 m); Height 19 ft. 7 in. (5.97 m).
Power Plant: Two Rolls Royce Avon 301 turbojet engines of 16,360 lb. (7,420 kg) thrust with afterburner.
Performance: Maximum Speed 1,386 mph (2,230 km/h) or Mach 2.1 at 36,000 ft. (10,975 m); Range (with ventral fuel tank) 800 miles (1,290 km).
Armament: Either two Red Top or two Firestreak air-to-air missiles on lower front fuselage, option for two 30 mm Aden cannons in forward part of ventral fuel tank, and underwing ordnance.

The Lightning represented a major step forward for the RAF when it entered squadron service at the start of the 1960's, being the RAF's first Mach 2-capable aircraft; its excellent climb performance and high speed have made it a very fine interceptor. It was also the first RAF aircraft designed as an integrated weapons system — its airframe, engines, armament, fire-control radar, and aircraft controls being specially integrated to create the best possible fighter layout. The Lightning also saw service with Saudi Arabia and Kuwait (with a ground attack capability) and will still equip some RAF squadrons until the Tornado F.Mk.2 enters service.

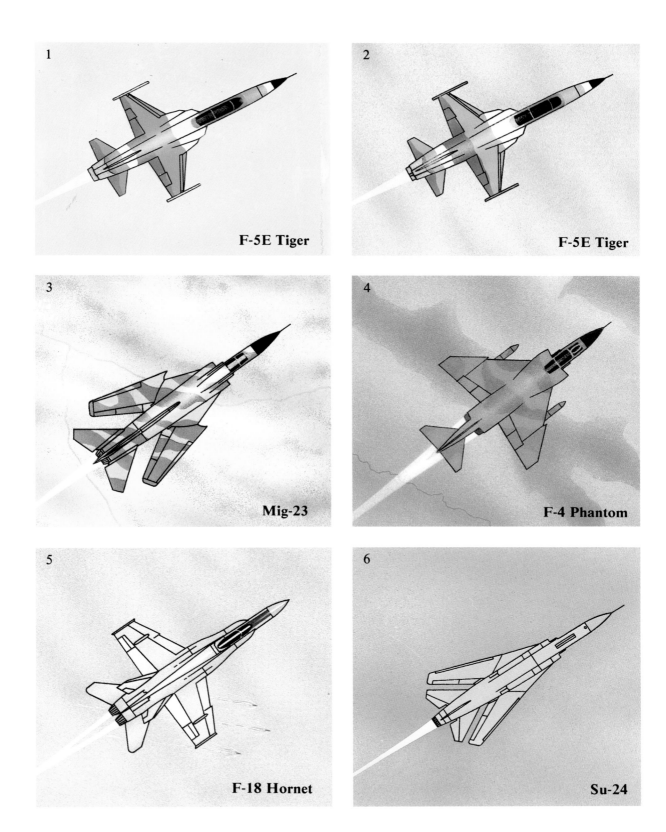

1   **F-5E Tiger**

2   **F-5E Tiger**

3   **Mig-23**

4   **F-4 Phantom**

5   **F-18 Hornet**

6   **Su-24**

15
Fighter Bases and Personnel

Fighter bases (see opposite page) contain the facilities necessary to keep the aircraft ready to carry out their missions. Specialist fire-fighting equipment is on stand-by to prevent damaged aircraft from catching fire when they land. During times of war, airfields can be important targets for the enemy to attack. Fighters need to be well-protected against attack on the ground, so many

The airfields at which fighters are based contain much specialized equipment. Highly skilled ground personnel at the bases keep the fighters in first-class condition to make sure that the aircraft are always ready to carry out the duties expected of them and are available for their pilots to fly whenever needed.

A fighter pilot wears clothing specially designed to enable him to operate efficiently in a very confined space. His one-piece jump-suit is more comfortable than a separate top and trousers and has many functional and safety attachments (illustrated): the multi-purpose connector links him up to various aircraft services such as the oxygen supply and intercom; perspex note pads are worn above the knee in a convenient position for checking pre-flight details and making in-flight notes; and his helmet (or bone-dome) has a sliding visor which can be used as a filter when he is flying into the sun.

The clothing must be suitable both for use inside the aircraft and for survival in an emergency, if the pilot has to eject himself from his aircraft or make a crash landing. In these circumstances, he will be thankful for his crash-helmet, warm gloves, heavy-duty flying suit, and flying boots. The quick-release mechanism instantly disconnects the pilot from all the aircraft services and leaves him equipped with every type of safety and survival device — a limited oxygen supply, inflatable Mae West with radio beacon and distress flares, a dinghy (clipped on to the seat while he is sitting down), and, of course, a parachute and emergency rations.

countries have built special hardened aircraft shelters on the airfields that protect the fighters. If an airfield's runways are put out of action during wartime, fighters in some countries are able to operate from strong sections of motorway or autobahn. The Harrier has a particular advantage over other fighters: with its V/STOL capability, it does not need runways to take off and land.

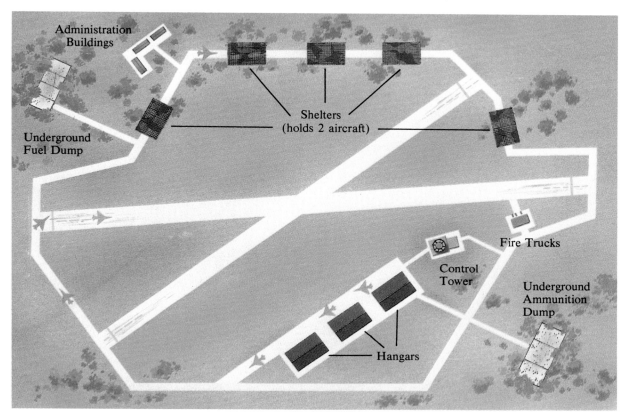

TOP FIGHTERS

Mikoyan-Gurevich MiG-21 "Fishbed"

Data for MiG-21 bis "Fishbed-N"

Dimensions: Span 7.15 m; Length (excluding nose probe) 15.10 m; Height 4.10 m.
Power Plant: One Tumansky R.25 turbojet engine of 7,500 kg thrust with afterburner.
Performance: Maximum Speed 2,285 km/h or Mach 2.15 above 11,000 m; Combat Radius (air-to-air mission with external fuel and four air-to-air missiles) 547 km.
Armament: One 23 mm GSh-23 cannon, up to 1,500 kg of air-to-ground weapons on four wing pylons, four AA-2-2 "Advanced Atoll" AAMs or two AA-2-2 and two AA-8 "Aphid" AAMs.

One of the most famous and widely used fighters of all time, the MiG-21 has served the Soviet air force for over two decades and has been widely exported to many countries around the world (see p. 42-3). Continuously updated to remain a capable front-line aircraft, it has successfully seen combat in such conflicts as the Vietnam war. The "Fishbed-N" is a third-generation derivative of the basic design, with a more powerful engine and improved avionics. The MiG-21 is well-liked by its pilots and still represents a great threat to more recent and advanced Western fighters.

16 Pilot Training (1)

Pilots go through a rigorous training before being qualified to fly the fighters of today. Pilot training is a long process of many months' duration, and this training costs a great deal of money.

Air forces have to ensure that only the applicants with the right abilities are chosen for fighter pilot training. Each applicant is put through a rigorous selection procedure before his proper training can begin. Although the period of selection is usually not very long, it attempts to ensure that the only applicants who can pass on to the actual training are the ones who are most likely to succeed in becoming fighter pilots.

The selection procedure usually consists of a variety of tests, interviews, and examinations. Among these are "aptitude" tests (1) to show if candidates have the necessary coordination to act quickly and correctly when faced with the changing problems likely to arise when flying high-speed fighters. Similarly, there are tests to discover good leadership qualities; a group of applicants is given a problem and in finding solutions it becomes obvious which candidates take the initiative.

As the interviews and tests progress, some of the original intake are found to be unsuitable to become fighter pilots, and the number of applicants is gradually reduced. Fighter pilots have to be physically fit, and each applicant has to pass full medical examinations.

Eventually, the remaining candidates pass on from the selection procedure into the training program itself. They are introduced to the various equipment that they will have to use when flying the fighter. If a fighter develops a fault or is hit in action, its pilot has to use his ejector seat to escape, so a ground simulator, like the one drawn (2), introduces the potential pilot to the kind of force he would be subjected to when an ejector seat is propelled out of an aircraft.

Only very few of the original applicants manage to pass all the phases of the selection procedure and training to become qualified fighter pilots. Some of those who fail to meet the requirements in the later stages of training might still become pilots, but of transport or similar aircraft. The diagram shows a typical intake of about 30 applicants of which only one or two will pass all the examinations and phases that enable them to join an operational fighter unit.

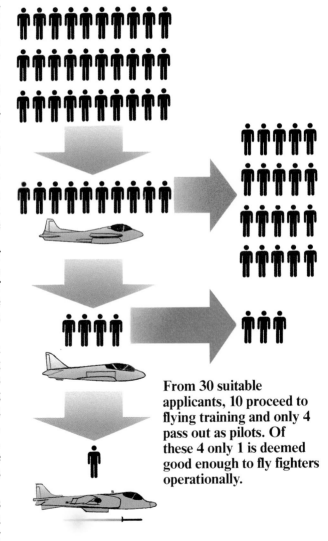

From 30 suitable applicants, 10 proceed to flying training and only 4 pass out as pilots. Of these 4 only 1 is deemed good enough to fly fighters operationally.

TOP FIGHTERS

Lockheed F-104 Starfighter

Data for F-104S Starfighter

Dimensions: Span (without wing-tip tanks) 6.68 m; Length 16.69 m; Height 4.11 m.
Power Plant: One General Electric J79-GE-19 turbojet engine of 8,120 kg thrust with afterburning.
Performance: Maximum Speed 2,330 km/h or Mach 2.2 at 11,000 m; Combat Radius (with maximum fuel) 1,247 km.
Armament: One 20 mm M61 cannon in fuselage, two Sparrow or Aspide medium-range AAMs and one Sidewinder AAM on each wing-tip or on underside pylons, provision for air-to-ground weapons on underside pylons.

For over a decade, the F-104 Starfighter remained as a singularly important fighter and ground attack aircraft within NATO, with many export customers being found for the type. Well over 2,000 Starfighters have been built. The F-104G accounts for a large number of these, being built by a massive international collaborative program including West Germany as a major partner. The original XF-104 prototype first flew in 1954, yet the type is still of great significance in several important air forces such as Canada and Italy. The current F-104S interceptor was built by Aeritalia in Italy even up to the late 1970's.

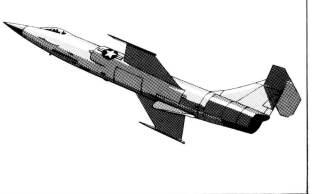

17 Pilot Training (2)

It is often many months into a pilot's training before he begins his actual flying training. Air forces have trainer aircraft in which pupil pilots are first introduced to flying. From then onwards, successful pupils fly more high performance types until they are passed as qualified to fly fighters.

Jet training aircraft usually have a two-seater layout. In the tandem layout shown in the drawing, the pupil sits in front of the instructor. The instructor's seat is raised above the pupil's allowing him the view forward to pilot the aircraft himself if necessary. Both sections of the cockpit are fitted with full flight instruments and controls. By the time that a trainee pilot has reached the end of his training and becomes fully qualified, he has probably spent around three years being trained. A great deal of his flying training is very expensive, often costing over $2 million.

When his training is complete, the pilot is fully qualified to fly fighters. A typical fighter cockpit is illustrated, and this is the type of often cramped but well-laid out cockpit that the fighter pilot flies in. It contains many instruments and displays that the pilot has to know intimately: especially in dog-fights, the pilot does not have time to waste examining his flight controls for a long time, so he must be able to use them properly without hesitating. Even when their training is complete, pilots continue to fly practice combats and missions to ensure that they are always ready to fly in action during wartime.

Hawk

TOP FIGHTERS

McDonnell Douglas F-15 Eagle

Dimensions: Span 13.05 m; Length 19.43 m; Height 5.63 m.
Power Plant: Two Pratt & Whitney F100-P-100 turbofan engines of 10,855 kg thrust with afterburner.
Performance: Maximum Speed 2,660 km/h or Mach 2.5 over 10,975 m; Combat Radius (air-to-air mission) 966 km.

Armament: One 20 mm M61 cannon beside starboard air intake, four Sparrow and four Sidewinder air-to-air missile, up to 7,258 kg of air-to-ground weapons.

The F-15 is widely regarded as the best fighter currently operating anywhere in the world. It carries an excellent mix of air-to-air weapons for interception as well as dog-fighting, while all versions can carry a considerable amount of attack weapons.

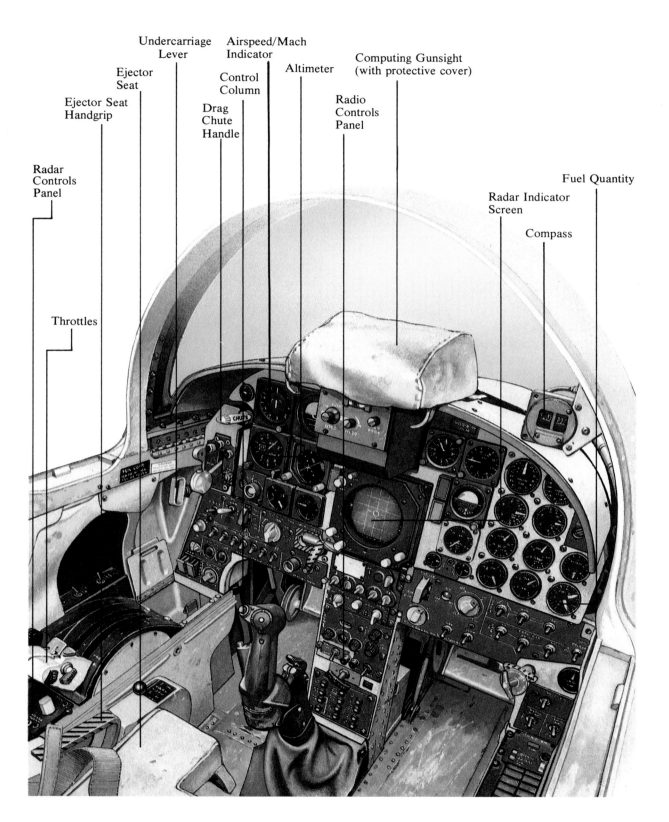

Radar
Controls
Panel

Ejector Seat
Handgrip

Ejector
Seat

Undercarriage
Lever

Airspeed/Mach
Indicator

Control
Column

Drag
Chute
Handle

Altimeter

Computing Gunsight
(with protective cover)

Radio
Controls
Panel

Fuel Quantity

Radar Indicator
Screen

Compass

Throttles

18 Fighter Cost and Distribution

Modern fighters are very expensive machines. Also very costly are the weapons that they use, together with the complicated avionics and other equipment that can be installed in them. This means that only the Superpowers and the richer countries can afford to build up really large forces of fighters. As fighters have become so complex and expensive, new ones are sometimes only developed and produced through multi-national cooperation. The Tornado, for example, shown on the front cover, has been developed jointly by Italy, Germany, and the United Kingdom by means of a

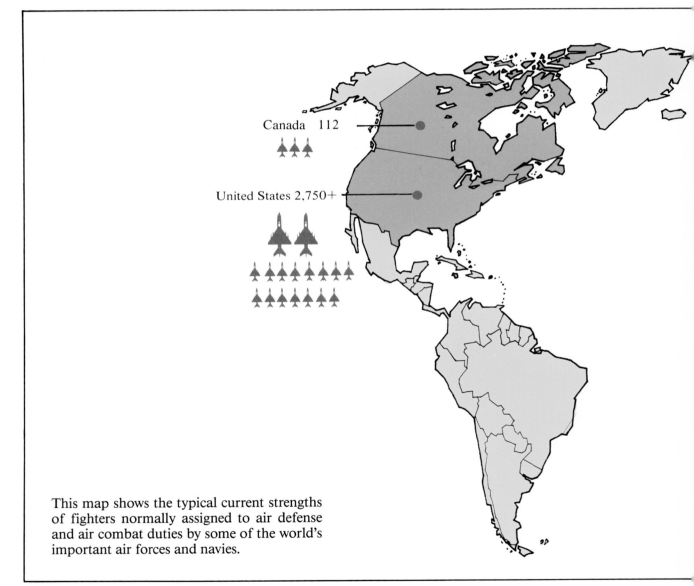

Canada   112

United States 2,750+

This map shows the typical current strengths of fighters normally assigned to air defense and air combat duties by some of the world's important air forces and navies.

tri-national company formed specially for its production.

Together with the fighter itself, it is necessary to buy the weapons that it needs to carry out its various missions, the radar to direct it to hostile aircraft, plus the equipment that the ground crews need to service the aircraft correctly. Proper airfields have to be built for the fighters to operate from, and aircraft carriers are required by those countries whose navies operate fighters. As explained on page 38, the training of pilots is also expensive.

Typically, a brand new U.S. Navy F-14 Tomcat interceptor costs $45.4 million. The price of the larger interceptors is generally much more than the smaller fighters employed mainly for dog-fighting, so that more of the smaller fighters can be bought by those air forces that have a limited budget for aircraft. The F-18 Hornet, for example, is smaller and lighter than the F-14 and costs around $28.1 million. In comparison, the 1944 price of a brand new North American P-51D Mustang, a very successful Second World War fighter, was just over $50,000.

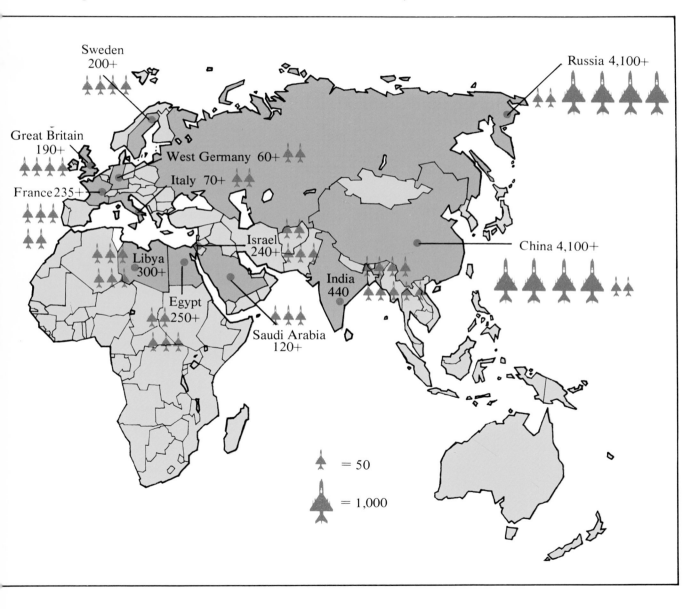

19 Fighters in Worldwide Service

The air forces of the Superpowers and other important countries are the major users of fighters, although many countries — both large and small — throughout the world operate fighters.

Some countries still operate fighters that the Superpowers have replaced years ago with more modern types. This is because the country involved cannot afford to replace them with modern fighters, or because it is friendly with its neighbors and therefore feels that it does not need more modern equipment. The fighters are supplied second-hand to these countries when the Air Forces of the Superpowers have retired them as front-line equipment.

Some Central American countries have continued employing North American P-51D Mustangs almost thirty years after the United States finished using them. Illustrated (below) is a Mustang of the Dominican Republic Air Force; the Dominican Republic is one of several countries that has used the Mustang for many years.

The Superpowers often export fighters to their major allies. The Russians have helped their friends in Eastern Europe, while many NATO countries of Western Europe have received American fighters. In addition, due to the cost of modern fighters, manufacturers in the larger countries find it useful to produce their fighters for export as this increases the sales of a particular type.

Sometimes, however, a friendly country that has been supplied with equipment suddenly becomes unfriendly and uses the fighters against the countries supplying them. An example of this is the Falkland Islands conflict when Argentina used French-supplied fighters against one of France's allies, Britain.

Occasionally, fighters provided by the opposing Superpowers are used in action against each other. The war between Iran and Iraq has seen Superpowers' equipment employed in this way: Iran using United States fighters, and Iraq flying mainly Russian fighters.

The chart shows the kind of export market throughout the world that the Superpowers can achieve with a successful fighter design.

MiG-21

Country	Number	
Soviet Union	1500+	▲ ✈✈✈✈✈✈✈✈✈✈
Czechoslovakia	300	✈✈✈✈✈✈
East Germany	200+	✈✈✈✈
North Korea	160	✈✈✈ ▴
Jugoslavia	100+	✈✈
Iraq	90	✈✈
Cuba	80	✈✈
Romania	150	✈✈✈
Vietnam	70	✈⊤
Bulgaria	60	✈ ▴
Ethiopia	60	✈ ▴
Afghanistan	40+	✈
Algeria	70	✈⊤
Poland	350+	✈✈✈✈✈✈✈
India	450+	✈✈✈✈✈✈✈✈✈
Finland	30+	✈
Egypt	350	✈✈✈✈✈✈✈
Hungary	100+	✈✈
Syria	200+	✈✈✈✈
Libya	94	✈✈

McDonnell Douglas F-4 Phantom II

Country	Number	
United States	3976	▲▲▲▲
West Germany	273	✈✈✈✈✈⊤
Iran	225	✈✈✈✈⊤
Israel	216+	✈✈✈✈⊤
Great Britain	182	✈✈✈⊤
Japan	156	✈✈✈ ▴
Turkey	80	✈✈
South Korea	73	✈⊤
Greece	64	✈⊤
Egypt	35	✈
Spain	40	✈

TOP FIGHTERS

Tupolev Tu-128 "Fiddler"

Data for Tu-128 "Fiddler"

Dimensions: Span 18.10 m; Length 27.20 m; Height 7.0 m.

Power Plant: Two Lyulka AL-21F-3 turbojet engines of 11,000 kg thrust with afterburner.

Performance: Maximum Speed, 1,900 km/h or Mach 1.8 above 11,000 m; Combat Radius (high altitude patrol with AAMs and fuel for supersonic interception) 1,255 km.

Armament: Four AA-5 "Ash" (two infra-red guided, two radar guided) air-to-air missiles below wings.

The Tu-128 is the largest and heaviest fighter ever to gain operational status anywhere in the world. The type has served with the Soviet Air Force's Air Defense Force for some twenty years. It is the ultimate heavy interceptor, carrying an extremely large long-range radar known in the West as "Big Nose," large air-to-air missiles, and two very powerful engines giving it a supersonic dash capability to intercept its targets.

20 Fighters in the Future

Current fighters are specially designed to accommodate all the latest advances in technology, but new inventions and ideas are arising that will greatly alter fighters in the future.

1

Anti-satellite Missions

The Superpowers are increasingly using space as a location for military equipment; spy satellites are just one of the many examples of this development. To counter this threat from space, it is planned to develop fighters to shoot down satellites. Special weapons are required to do this, and at present the U.S. Air Force intends to use the F-15 Eagle (see page 8) to release them. The weapon is launched after the aircraft has climbed vertically upwards at full power (1). Such a launch method is especially useful for satellites in a high orbit above the Earth, even though the fighter itself does not enter space.

New Designs Under Development

Because they have a large number of flat surfaces and sharp angles, current fighters are easily detected by radar. Stealth aircraft are now being designed to counteract this. With as many curved surfaces as possible, the stealth fighter offers few detectable areas for radar to pick up (2).

Another design possibility is forward-swept wings; these create less drag at high speeds so the aircraft can travel faster with less power (3). At low speeds, the fighter is generally easier to control than ordinary aircraft. The wings could be controlled by computers to enable the planes to make extremely fast, tight turns that would tear today's aircraft to pieces. Great advances are being made with fighter engines; in the future, they will be much more powerful and yet far lighter than at present and will have dramatically reduced fuel consumption.

The current V/STOL Harrier can only fly at subsonic speeds. It is now being re-designed to carry much heavier loads and to fly at supersonic speeds. The new aircraft will be built using a special new carbon-epoxy material that is stronger and yet much lighter than the metals currently used in the construction of fighters. Eventually, these composite materials will be used in all future fighters.

TOP FIGHTERS

Panavia Tornado

Data for Tornado F.Mk.2

Dimensions: Span (wings fully swept-back) 8.59 m, (wings fully spread) 13.90 m; Length (excluding nose pitot) 18.06 m; Height 5.70m.
Power Plant: Two Turbo-Union RB.199 Mk.103 turbofan engines of 7,258 kg thrust with afterburner.
Performance: Maximum Speed over 2,414 km/h or Mach 2.27 above 10,975 m; Combat Radius (Combat Air Patrol mission with 2 hours' loiter and fuel for ten minutes combat) over 644 km.

Armament: One 27 mm Mauser cannon in front fuselage, four Sky Flash medium-range AAMs recessed under fuselage and two Sidewinder dog-fighting missiles.

The Tornado is produced jointly by Britian, West Germany, and Italy and was designed as a multi-role combat aircraft that has main roles of strike missions against ground targets and air-to-air interception missions. The Tornado F.Mk.2 is the RAF interceptor version that, from 1984, replaces Lightnings and eventually Phantoms in defending the vast areas of airspace around Britain. Its powerful Foxhunter radar can find targets at over 115 mile (185 km) range, but the aircraft also carries Sidewinder missiles for dog-fighting and close combat.

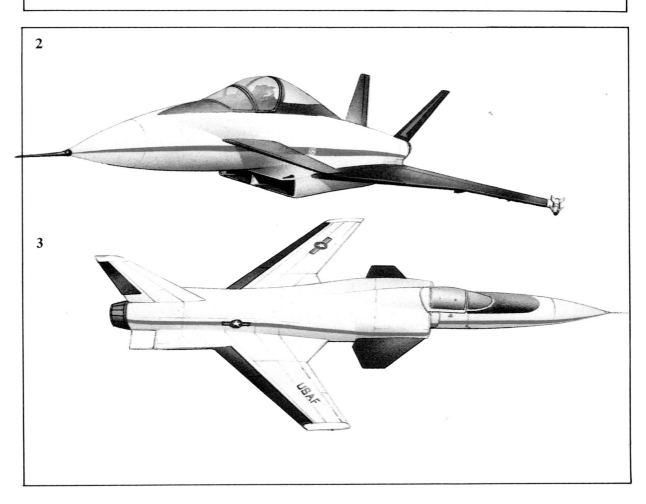

2

3

Glossary

AAM
Air-to-Air Missile

AFTERBURNER
In order to dramatically increase the power given out by jet engines for short periods such as take-off or for fast speed bursts, fuel is injected directly into the hot jet stream as it leaves the engine's turbine (See Turbojet/Turbofan), producing additional thrust. This after-burning consumes a great deal of fuel, hence its use for short periods only.

AIM
Air Intercept Missile, the U.S. designation for AAMs including the AIM-7 Sparrow, the AIM-9 Sidewinder series, and the AIM-54 Phoenix

ARMEE DE L'AIR
The French air force

AVIONICS
(from *avi*ation electr*onics*), the science concerned with the development of electronics and electrical devices for use in aircraft. The term is sometimes used generally, to embrace the aircraft's electronic and cockpit equipment and displays.

AWACS
Airborne Warning and Control System, the name given to aircraft fitted with a vast array of radar, surveillance, and communications equipment that provide an airborne radar picture of a large area of sky and relay information to friendly aircraft and forces about the movements of hostile aircraft

BAE
British Aerospace, the British nationalized aircraft company created from several formerly independent companies during the 1970s

ECM
Electronic Counter Measures, the science of investigating and then jamming, confusing, or otherwise disturbing an enemy's radars and related electronic equipment by mainly electronic means

F-
Fighter, in the US system of designation to indicate the type and role of a particular warplane. The now current F- series was instituted in 1962, from which time all US Navy and Air Force fighters have been designated under the same system, including such famous types as the Navy F-14 Tomcat and the Air Force F-15 Eagle. The F naming system is also used in the West to describe Soviet warplanes: all code-names for Soviet fighters beginning with the letter "F," such as the Su-15 "Flagon" and the MiG-21 "Fishbed."

FAST
Fuel And Sensor Tactical pack, a large streamlined external fuel pallet available for fitting to the F-15's air intake sides to increase range

FLY-BY-WIRE
Method of controlling an aircraft in which the normal control rods and actuators needed to move the control surfaces are replaced by electrical channels that relay instructions to the control surfaces by electrical impulses and signals. This saves much weight and allows the aircraft to fly even in an unstable condition, its computers issuing control instructions that keep it in the air and can also help to aid the fighter's agility in dog-fighting.

GE
General Electric, a leading U.S. designer and manufacturer of aircraft engines

HUD
Head-Up Display, the cockpit instrument that projects all relevant flight and weapon-aiming details into the pilot's line of sight to prevent him from having to repeatedly look down at his normal flight instruments

IFF
Identification Friend/Foe, an airborne interrogating device aimed at telling between the electronic and other signals of friendly or hostile aircraft

MiG (MIKOYAN GUREVICH)
A Soviet designer and manufacturer of several important and successful fighter designs

NATO
North Atlantic Treaty Organization, a body arising from a 1949 treaty guaranteeing mutal assistance and military cooperation. Altogether it contains fifteen countries (although France is not in the military command structure) of Western Europe and North America.

P (OR P&W)
Pratt & Whitney, a very important aircraft engine company in the U.S.

PORT
Left-hand

RADAR
(from *ra*dio *de*tection *a*nd *ra*nging), the electronic system that can detect an aircraft hidden by darkness, distance, or cloud cover, by the transmission of extremely high-frequency radio pulses, which are reflected back to the transmitter by the aircraft and thus show its distance, position, and speed. Radar can also be used in such instances as controlling AAMs to their targets over long distances.

SNECMA
Sociètè Nationale d'Etude et de Construction de Moteurs d'Aviation, a French designer and manufacturer of aircraft engines

STARBOARD
Right-hand

SU (SUKHOI)
A Soviet fighter and attack aircraft manufacturer and designer

SUPERPOWERS
A term usually applied to the U.S. and the Soviet Union

TU (TUPOLEV)
A Soviet designer and manufacturer of mainly bomber aircraft, although Tupolev also created the world's largest operational fighter — the Tu-128

TURBOJET/TURBOFAN
The turbojet is a jet engine in which a turbine-driven compressor draws in air at the engine air intake at the front of the engine and forces the compressed air into a combustion chamber. Fuel is injected into this chamber and then ignited, the hot gases so produced subsequently rushing through and driving the turbine and then being ejected at the outlet nozzle at the rear. Forward thrust is created as a reaction to the rearward momentum of the exhaust gases. This type of engine has a quite high fuel consumption. A more recent development is the turbofan, which is significantly different in that some of the in-coming air is by-passed around the combustion chamber and accelerated rearwards by a turbine-operated fan to mix with the exhaust gases from the combustion chamber. This increases the air-mass flowing rearwards over that achieved in the turbojet, increasing thrust without increasing fuel consumption.

VIFF
Vectoring In Forward Flight. The method by which the Harrier and Sea Harrier use their specially swivelling engine nozzles, which normally give them the ability to take off vertically and then change to normal forward flight, to gain advantages of increased maneuverability in dog-fighting

VTOL
Vertical Take-Off and Landing

Index

V/STOL
Vertical/Short Take-Off and Landing, in which the aircraft can take off and land vertically but can also (like the Harrier) perform a conventional but short rolling take-off

WARSAW PACT
A mutual defense organization created in 1955 between the Communist countries of Eastern Europe. It provides a unified military command among the member countries and allows Soviet units to be stationed inside the borders of the other members; the organization is an equivalent of NATO.

WILD WEASEL
Often a converted fighter like the F-4G Phantom version, the Wild Weasel is specially fitted for the air-to-ground role, carrying ECM equipment and weapons for jamming or destroying an enemy's defense and radar installations.